History Is

RiCH

Written by Shaun S. Nichols
Drawn by Sophy Smith

First published 2022.
Printed in China.

HONEST HISTORY CO.
PO Box 451973
Los Angeles, CA 90045
@honesthistory

DESIGN
Carly Barton

EDITOR
Theresa Kay

10 9 8 7 6 5 4 3 2 1
ISBN 978 1 7361919 4 1

ABOUT THE AUTHOR

Shaun S. Nichols is an Assistant Professor of History at Boise State University. He previously taught at Harvard University, where he received his Ph.D. in 2016. His research and teaching center on the economic history of the United States and the world. He has published articles and reviews for *Enterprise & Society*, *Labor*, and the *Business History Review*. He is currently working on a book manuscript, *Crisis Capital: Industrial Massachusetts and the Making of Global Capitalism, 1813–Present*, which explores the complex history of American industrialization and deindustrialization.

AUTHOR'S ACKNOWLEDGMENTS

For this academic historian, writing a book with no footnotes was a liberating, humbling, and at times painful experience. After all, with each sentence—lacking the ability to leave behind the standard trail of citations—I felt a pang of guilt in skipping over all the fantastic work and talented scholars who made a book like this possible! *History Is Rich* draws on the research of countless historians—too many to name. In crafting this book, I found myself especially thinking back to the excellent work of Edward Baptist, Sven Beckert, Alan Brinkley, Colin Calloway, Alfred Chandler, Christopher Clark, Dorothy Sue Cobble, Lizabeth Cohen, Jefferson Cowie, William Cronon, Christine Desan, Thomas Dublin, Eric Foner, Chris Friday, Tera Hunter, Joseph Inikori, Alice Kessler-Harris, James Kloppenberg, Naomi Lamoreaux, Walter Licht, Nancy Maclean, Drew McCoy, Thomas K. McCraw, Edmund Morgan, Sharon Ann Murphy, Johann Neem, Nell Irvin Painter, Daniel Rodgers, Andrew Shankman, Judith Stein, Richard White, and Gordon S. Wood. I also owe a special thanks to all of my outstanding colleagues in the History Department at Boise State University— especially Lisa Brady, who encouraged me to pursue this particular project. My editor at Honest History, Brooke Knight, was a joy to work with and make this book infinitely better. Finally, I owe a special thanks to my wife, Katy, who continues to (somehow) support my love of history.

I cannot imagine any historian mentioned here will agree with every word I wrote, but they were all in some way on my mind in crafting this narrative. I owe them all a debt of gratitude. With that debt in mind, I gratefully dedicate this book to the teachers, professors, and educators who guided me on my journey. I hope they all know what an enormous difference they made in my life.

that goal. But the passion that citizens bring to these debates is a sign of how deeply we care about our nation—and, hopefully, one another.

History is rich. It is also always changing. What will happen next? The answer is largely up to you. One of the most incredible things about democracy is that we get to decide, together, what future we want to pursue. So, as you go through life and observe our economy in action, think about which (if any!) of these economic ideas seems most compelling to you. Chances are, you will one day be in a voting booth deciding which set of ideas you would like to see enacted!

TABLE OF CONTENTS

INTRODUCTION

What is the point of learning about history?

Many Americans think of historians as people obsessed with the past: people who dedicate their lives to memorizing dates and names. They imagine historians as those who are fascinated by the small details of "what happened": stuffy, bearded professors who preoccupy themselves with how many buttons were on the uniform of a French officer's jacket in the 1870s… or the trivial details of the Taft presidency.

There is some truth to this. Without a doubt, historians do care about the past. But, it may surprise you to learn that what historians *really* care about is the *present*. Historians are *actually* obsessed with the present.

That may seem hard to believe. But, remember, most historians only study the past because what we *really* want to understand is our own time. It is just that historians are convinced that the only way to understand our world today is to understand *how we got here*. If you want to understand our politics, you need to understand how our politics developed. If you want to understand our society, you need to understand how it formed. And, if you want to understand our current economy, then you have to learn how and why our economy came together in the way it did.

When a historian sits in the archive rummaging through leftover boxes of documents from the Pennsylvania Railroad, they may seem lost in the past. In reality, they are trying to figure out crucial questions about the present.

What are corporations, and where did they come from? How does the stock market work? How does any market work? How did America become such a rich nation? Why are some in America still, nonetheless, so poor? What role does the government play in our economy?

Questions like these fascinate economic historians. And, considering how important the economy is in making sure each and every one of us (hopefully) leads a happy, prosperous life with a fulfilling job—these questions should fascinate you too! For historians, the only way to answer these questions is to search the past.

This is the mission of this book. It is the story of the American economy. It is a story of many failures and successes. It is a story of many people and ideas. Founding fathers, enslaved African Americans, Native tribes, wealthy industrialists, high-flying bankers, overworked factory laborers, big-name political leaders, and genius innovators all play a role in this story. Together, these Americans (and countless others) made our economy what it is today.

Let's dive in!

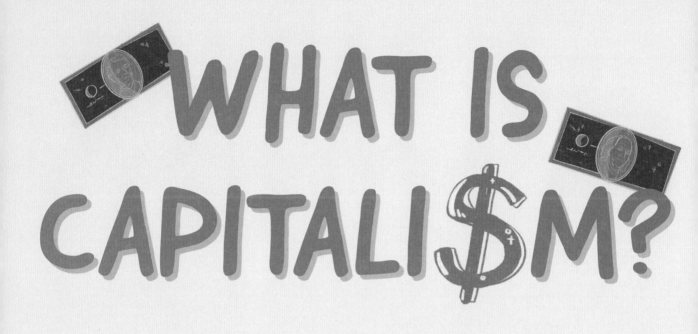

WHAT IS CAPITALI$M?

In this book, we are going to learn about money, wealth, and the making of the American economy. To do this, we need to understand a complicated word: "capitalism."

What is capitalism? It is the system that defines the rules of the American economy. To understand how our economy works, we need to first understand how capitalism works.

CAPITALISM IS DEFINED BY THREE KEY CHARACTERISTICS:

1. PRIVATE OWNERSHIP

2. PROFIT

3. COMPETITIVE MARKETPLACE

PRIVATE OWNERSHIP

In a capitalist economy, things and lands are owned by individual people, businesses, or the government. Property is "privately" owned when it is only for the use of its owner.

PROFIT

Under capitalism, business owners want to make a profit. In other words, they want to earn money by selling what they produce. Often, this involves *investment*. Investment is when someone spends money to (hopefully!) make *more* money in the future. Let's say you are getting ready for a big bake sale. If you go to the store and spend money on the ingredients to make brownies to sell, you are *investing* in your brownie business. You are buying ingredients *now* because you want to make more money *later* by selling brownies.

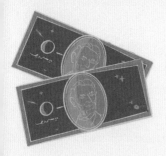
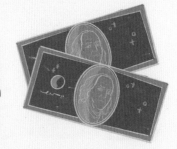

COMPETITIVE MARKETPLACE

How do your brownies end up in the hands of customers? Under capitalism, individuals are supposed to freely *compete* to gain the things they want by buying them. They also profit by selling the products that they make. This is how a market works.

This competition takes many forms. Businesses must compete against other businesses. You might want to sell your brownies for $20 a slice. That could make you a lot of money. But there is a problem with this plan. There are other sellers at the bake sale, and their brownies will likely be a lot cheaper. Customers will buy brownies from them instead. Competition forces you to sell for a more reasonable price.

Consumers must also compete against other consumers. Imagine instead that hundreds of customers show up to the bake sale, but you are the only vendor! Now, there is a lot of *demand* for brownies (lots of hungry customers) but a low *supply* of brownies (you are the only vendor who showed up!). Hungry customers will have to compete against other hungry customers to get a brownie. When smart businesses see this, they often raise their prices. Maybe you *can* charge $20 a slice. You are their only option!

This is what economists mean when they say that supply and demand determine prices. You can see it all around you if you know what to look for. When an item is in low supply but in high demand, it tends to fetch a high price (think: diamonds or rare baseball cards). When an item is in high supply with low demand, it tends to have a low price (think: used clothing or expired tuna).

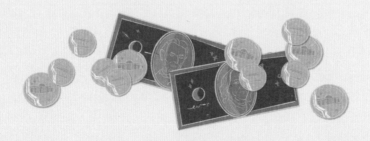

WHAT ROLE SHOULD THE GOVERNMENT PLAY IN A CAPITALIST SYSTEM?

This question is hotly debated! Some Americans think the government should play a limited role in our economy. They say that the capitalist economy is best left to its own devices. Others disagree. They point out that there are certain key services and functions that the government *has* to provide for the economy to work. For instance, how do roads get paid for in a competitive market system? Who pays for them? The answer is not clear. (Imagine if every time you used any section of road you had to stop and pay the road's owner a dollar. That would slow down traffic!) So, instead of relying on a market for our roads, maybe it is better to pay taxes and have the government build free roads for everybody.

As we will see, from Thomas Jefferson and Alexander Hamilton up to today, these questions over what role (and how big of a role) the government should play in the economy have made for some of the oldest debates in American history.

The Beginnings of the
AMERICAN ECONOMY

Today, capitalism might seem like "just the way the world works." But before capitalism, most economies looked different. To see this, we don't need to look further than the Native inhabitants of what we now think of as the United States. These nations maintained economies based on kinship, trade, and gift exchange. In other words, most Native nations produced or gathered resources together, and these goods were often shared among the group.

THE GOAL WAS NOT INDIVIDUAL PROFIT OR GAIN, BUT EVERYONE'S SURVIVAL.

Take, for instance, the Native Americans of what we now call the plains of the Midwest. A major source of food for these Native nations, aside from farming, was buffalo. Before the introduction of horses by Europeans, groups of 100 to 150 men would hunt buffalo by trying to funnel herds  toward a cliff. Using everything from blankets to spears, they would then try to excite the buffalo to stampede over the cliff to their deaths. The food and skins this brought would be shared with the entire group.

These early Native economic systems are sometimes called "gift economies." In a "gift economy," the exchange of goods does not happen through buying and selling in a competitive marketplace, but by building relationships through the exchange of gifts. The Native nations of what we now call the Pacific Northwest, for instance, also hunted and gathered in groups and shared in the takings. An important ceremony for these groups was the Potlach, an event at which leaders would give away or even destroy goods as a way of cementing their high status. In a capitalist society, like ours, people often want to gain as much as they can—people want to get rich! But for these Native nations, giving away possessions was a way of building relationships and strengthening their communities.

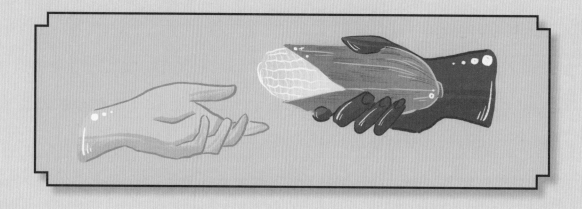

The European powers who ventured out to the Americas had different ideas about the economy. Too often, we imagine that Europeans came to the Americas in search of religious liberty, exploration, or new lands for settlement. More accurately, Europeans ventured to the Americas with largely economic desires in mind. Their goals were resources, riches, and profit.

Some powers, such as Spain and Portugal, found exactly this. These empires conquered and plundered the rich resources of Central and South America. Other powers, including England, found riches much harder to come by, at least at first. In fact, the first batch of

colonists at Jamestown, Virginia, the first permanent English settlement in the Americas, planted few food crops when they arrived. They assumed that, like the Spanish before them, they would find plenty of gold—gold that they could trade with others for food. This was a ghastly error. They found no gold, and starvation soon overtook the colony.

> ## ONLY ONE-THIRD OF THE JAMESTOWN COLONISTS SURVIVED THE FIRST WINTER.

Eventually, with the introduction of tobacco agriculture, England found a way to profit from its Virginia colonies. The same cannot be said of their colonies in New England. With hot and humid summers and cold, brutal winters, there seemed to be few opportunities for profit in New England. As a result, the area did indeed become a magnet for England's religious minorities and those in search of agricultural land—but only because it seemed to have no other productive use!

The relationship between these English colonists and the Native peoples of America was always a difficult one. Waves of European disease (to which these Native Americans had never been exposed) killed millions, weakening these groups before Europeans even drew a weapon. At times, English colonists and certain nations engaged in relatively friendly trade. Some nations even occasionally allied with English colonists. But, quite often, as the English expanded their presence in America, conflict erupted between growing English colonies and settled Native communities.

Economic life in the English colonies looked different depending on where you stood. In the northern colonies, despite the harsh climate, settlers tried their best to support themselves through agriculture. In the south, colonists began growing tobacco to sell to Europeans. It was on this foundation that, in 1776, the United States was born. One of the first tasks of that young nation was to figure out what shape its economy should take.

THE FOUNDING FATHERS & THE AMERICAN ECONOMY

Too often, we learn in school that the "founding fathers"—the American revolutionaries who created the political foundations of our nation—basically agreed about everything. We learn that they all believed in freedom, equality, justice, and democracy. But that does not tell the whole story.

The founders often disagreed furiously over how to achieve these goals. And some of the most heated debates of this era centered on the future of the American economy. They involved two very different leaders: Thomas Jefferson and Alexander Hamilton.

Although Hamilton never served as president (Jefferson did from 1801 to 1809), he was a chief economic advisor to our nation's first president, George Washington. Hamilton pushed some radical ideas. He dreamed of the United States becoming a great industrial nation. He wanted to create a strong national government that could use tariffs (taxes on goods we buy from other countries) and a permanent national debt (money our nation owes to others) to help fund manufacturing companies.

THE UNITED STATES SHOULD BE AN INDUSTRIAL NATION!

HAMILTON

For Hamilton's supporters, who formed a political party called the "Federalists" in 1791, this seemed like a bold plan for our country to become a great military and economic power. For other Americans, it seemed like Hamilton wanted to give away money to those who were already very wealthy.

Thomas Jefferson and James Madison, who opposed Hamilton's ideas, created their own political party in 1792, which would eventually become today's "Democratic Party." For Jefferson, the American Revolution was fought for freedom and democracy. He imagined that Americans were truly free when they could establish themselves as independent, land-owning farmers. In 1785, Jefferson wrote,

> *"THOSE WHO LABOR IN THE EARTH ARE THE CHOSEN PEOPLE OF GOD...WHILE WE HAVE LAND TO LABOR THEN, LET US NEVER WISH TO SEE OUR CITIZENS OCCUPIED AT A WORK-BENCH."*

For Jefferson, Hamilton's dream of an industrial America was more of a nightmare. He feared that in Hamilton's America, citizens would be removed from the freedom of the farm, pushed into factories, and forced to do whatever a boss told them to do.

Jefferson worried Hamilton's economic plans might destroy democracy itself. Remember, a democracy means that everybody gets a say in what our government does. But it can be difficult for our government to act when people disagree over what it should do. Even today, farmers, workers, factory owners, landlords, renters, and bankers will often push for different goals. Jefferson hoped a democracy of simple farmers would avoid these problems. He thought that farmers would largely agree on what was good for everybody. That would make it easier for a democratic government to work.

Jefferson's pro-farmer policies, including his support for westward expansion and low tariffs, also benefited another major group of Americans: slaveowners. Although Jefferson often spoke out against slavery, he himself owned slaves. He was also supported by many American slaveholders.

THE UNITED STATES SHOULD BE A DEMOCRACY OF FARMERS!

JEFFERSON

How might you have voted in these early days of our nation? Farms and factories, democracy and division: these are debates we are still having today!

SLAVERY AND THE AMERICAN ECONOMY

It may surprise you to learn that, in the eyes of European explorers and colonists, the lands that now make up the American east coast seemed a terrible disappointment. Spanish conquerors in Central and South America had found cities of gold and silver to plunder. Portuguese Brazil became a land of precious metals, diamonds, and sugar plantations.

In contrast, it seemed like our nation had nothing of much value. A new settler in New England found no gold or diamonds—just a lot of snowy winters and rocky soils!

THREE INGREDIENTS WERE CENTRAL TO REVERSING OUR ECONOMIC FORTUNES:

TOBACCO, COTTON, AND, MOST IMPORTANTLY, SLAVERY.

As early as 1612, Virginia settlers were beginning to plant tobacco. By the late 1660s, they were growing 15 million pounds of it each year. Virginia soon became the most important supplier of tobacco to Western Europe.

But there was a problem. The work was brutally hard. Waves of disease would take the lives of about half the new arrivals each summer. Few people were willing to volunteer for such an ordeal. So...Who would do the hard work of farming?

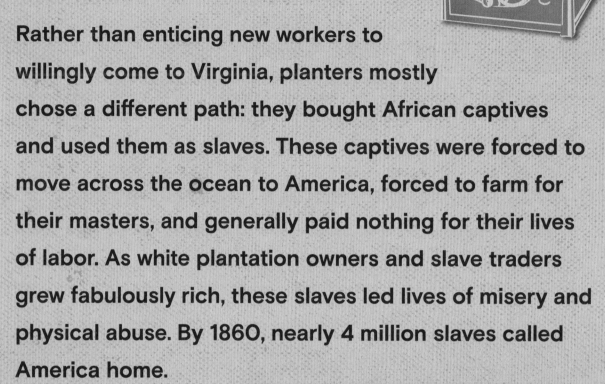

Rather than enticing new workers to willingly come to Virginia, planters mostly chose a different path: they bought African captives and used them as slaves. These captives were forced to move across the ocean to America, forced to farm for their masters, and generally paid nothing for their lives of labor. As white plantation owners and slave traders grew fabulously rich, these slaves led lives of misery and physical abuse. By 1860, nearly 4 million slaves called America home.

Slavery was also critical to another crop that stood at the center of the American economy for about 50 years: cotton. In fact, by

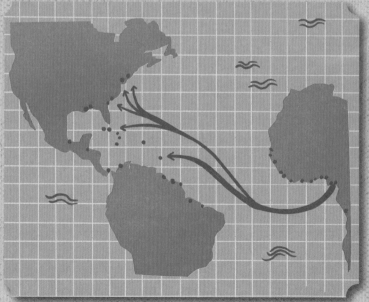

1860, the United States was producing enough cotton each year to fill up the Empire State Building three times over! America became the world's leading cotton producer.

Most white Americans accepted slavery, at least at first. After all, slavery was turning America into a wealthy and important global power. In addition, many whites clung to a totally false belief in their own "racial superiority." In other words, they believed that white people deserved to be masters, and black people deserved to be slaves. Over time, however, a rising group of Americans—the Abolitionists—began to protest the slave system on both moral and religious grounds.

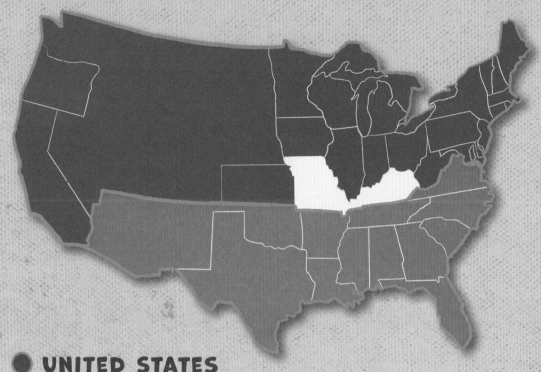

● **UNITED STATES**
○ **BORDER STATES**
◐ **CONFEDERATE STATES**

As Southerners grew nervous that this rising Northern anti-slavery movement might topple their vicious economic system, 11 southern states abruptly left (seceded from) the United States, starting in 1860. So began the American Civil War (1861–1865). Over two million northerners (including 179,000 black men) and one million southerners would battle over the future of slavery and the preservation of our nation.

Southern defeat brought many changes to the American economy. Although African Americans would long continue to experience discrimination, violence, and a basic lack of equal rights, the Civil War finally put an end to the terrible system of slavery. Additionally, with the American government in the hands of northern, pro-industrial politicians, new laws were passed encouraging industrial development, railroad expansion, and western agriculture. The effects of these changes were enormous. An economy based primarily on slavery and southern agriculture would soon be transformed into one centered on northeastern industry and westward expansion.

THE INDUSTRIAL REVOLUTION

It may seem surprising that the world's first factories were created to produce cotton cloth and yarn (textiles). But clothing is an item that every human being needs. Because of this, there were people around the globe who wanted to buy machine-made cloth. Cotton was the main raw resource necessary to produce cloth. It was being produced in huge volumes by southern slaves.

> ## THERE WAS ONE BIG PROBLEM, THOUGH. AMERICA DID NOT HAVE THE NECESSARY MACHINE TECHNOLOGY.

Textile factories had started in Britain in 1771. They used giant machines powered by the moving water of nearby rivers to spin yarn. These machines eventually weaved cloth. For a time, Britain was the only industrial power in the world. The British government even stopped textile workers from emigrating abroad. They wanted the technology to stay in Britain.

As a result, the American Industrial Revolution began with an act of industrial espionage. The story starts with Samuel Slater. Born in 1768 in Derbyshire, England, Slater began working in local factories at the age of 10. By the time he was 21 years old, he had learned all about textile production. He knew that America was interested in manufacturing—the tale goes—so Slater disguised himself as a farmer and left

England. On his arrival in the United States, he formed a partnership with two Rhode Island merchants. By 1793, they had founded the first American factory: the Slater Mill. From there, factories and machines spread all over the nation.

In America, Slater became the "Father of the American Factory System." In Britain, he was "Slater the Traitor"!

"SLATER THE TRAITOR"!

But Americans were not always excited about these new factories. Many people, especially adult men, did not want to give up a life of independent farming to take orders from a boss and work behind a machine all day. Because of this, America's earliest factory workers were mostly children, young women, and new immigrants. The first manufacturing workers at Slater's Mill, for instance, were seven boys and two girls, all 12 years old or younger.

History is rarely just good or bad. This is true for the Industrial Revolution. "Industrialization" was not without its problems. The key ingredient in many of these early factories, cotton, was grown by enslaved workers. American factory workers in the 1800s often lived in poverty and worked long hours. Those who worked in the mills, including children,

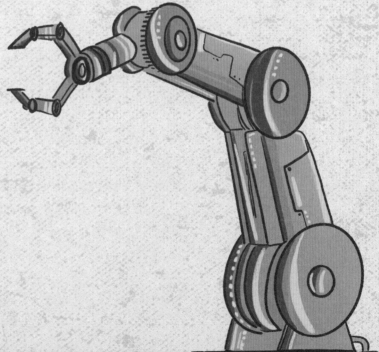

often worked 12 or 14 hours each day. Industrial work was hard and repetitive. Many factories spewed pollutants into America's air and water.

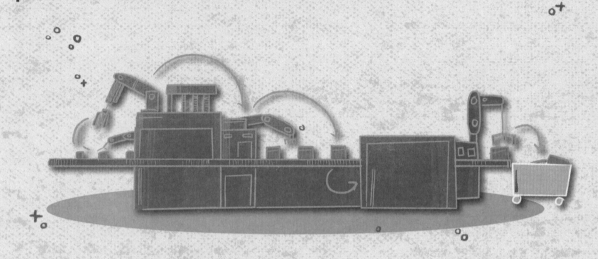

But these factories also did many good things, too. The economy grew. American factories may have started by producing cotton cloth, but they expanded. Soon they were churning out all sorts of new products: steel, automobiles, chemicals, and corn flakes! All of these new manufactured goods were soon available to everyday Americans. It is likely that you are right now surrounded by all sorts of incredible machine-made products, including this book!

As a result, much of American economic history since the 1800s has been about trying to get the best of both worlds. Many laws and regulations have since been passed with the aim of preserving the good parts of the Industrial Revolution (amazing new products!) while avoiding some of these downsides (such as pollution and poverty).

MONEY AND BANKING

By the end of the 1800s, business was *booming* in America. To understand that boom, we need to understand how *money* and *banking* were changing in this time period.

MONEY

Human societies have often tried to find an object that could serve as a general form of payment for goods: in other words, money. The hope was to find objects with a high value in a small package. For this reason, hard metals such as gold and silver have frequently been used in money systems. There is really nothing "special" about chunks of gold or silver: they are just things that happen to have a high value and can easily fit in your pocket!

Many money systems have existed throughout American history. In fact, from 1837 to 1863, we went through a period of "free banking," in which multiple paper currencies floated around the nation. Banks, stores, railroads, and everyday businesses could issue their own paper money. Some paper money was good. Some was worthless. A lot of money (about a third) was phony. As a result, if you were an American traveling around the country, it would usually be easier to spend metal coins issued by a foreign country (say, a silver British pound or a gold French Franc) than paper money from your hometown!

During the early 1860s, amid the Civil War, the United States finally adopted a national banking system and a uniform currency. This development helped grow industry and expand the American marketplace.

Until the 1970s, the value of that money was "backed" by precious metals in the US treasury. In other words, for every American dollar in circulation, there was a dollar of gold or silver sitting in a government storehouse that could be potentially exchanged for that dollar. Since 1971, however, the United States has relied entirely on what is called "fiat money." This is just a fancy way of saying that US paper money today has value because

(A) the government mandates it can be used to pay taxes and debt, and (B) people generally think it has value. Believe it or not, this is the real foundation of the "value" of American money today!

BANKS

Most Americans think of "banks" as a place that stores money. If you put $100 in the bank on Monday, you can withdraw $20 on Thursday to buy an overpriced brownie at a bake sale. For most consumers, this is what a bank does.

But the real function of a bank is to *lend money*. Banks take in deposits, yes, but only because they then loan most of what is deposited. Why? Because these loans come with *interest*—basically, an extra amount somebody must pay for the privilege of borrowing money. (Imagine your friend loans you $10 for lunch, but then your friend says they want $11 when you pay them back. You just got charged 10% in interest!) This is how a bank makes money.

It is hard to overstate the importance of these loans in history. Most businesses require a lot of upfront money (initial investment) to get off the ground. Railroads, in particular, required tremendous amounts of money to get built.

For this reason, banks played a huge role in the economic development of the United States.

But—remember— where do banks get all that money for lending? From

FARMER GIVES BANK $100. BANK KEEPS $10 AND LOANS THE OTHER $90.

deposits! So, like it or not, when you put $100 in the bank, the bank does not put your money in a special

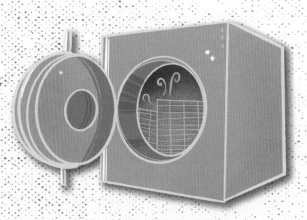

box with your name on it. Instead, most of the money is loaned out, and only a small portion (about $10, usually) is kept in the bank's vault.

HOW CAN THAT POSSIBLY WORK?

How is it that banks can survive if they are loaning out 90% of what is deposited each day? Simply put, it is rare that every depositor shows up at the exact same time to withdraw every cent they have in the bank.

Yet, especially during moments of economic distress, this is exactly what happens. Everybody rushes to the bank to withdraw their money. This is called a "bank run." At that point, banks can (and do) collapse. This is exactly what happened during the Great Depression, for instance. Thankfully, reforms since the Great Depression now protect average Americans from losing money in the (rare) event of a bank failure.

RAILROADS AND BIG BUSINESS

After the Civil War, the United States transformed into a major industrial power. In 1860, the United States was still behind Britain, Germany, and France in industrial output. By 1900, US industry was zooming past these three rivals put together. This era is sometimes referred to as the "Second Industrial Revolution."

The "First" Industrial Revolution was centered mainly on cotton textiles, but the "Second" Industrial Revolution was driven by heavy manufacturing. This included steel, chemicals, electronics, and the railroad. Only 9,000 miles of rail spanned the United States in 1850. By 1900, there were nearly 200,000 miles of rail. That much railroad could have circled the earth's equator almost 8 times!

Railroads changed the nation. Most importantly, they connected the farms, mines, and forests of the American west with the hungry factories (and hungry factory workers!) of the American east. The rails were used to ship Texas oil, Pacific Northwest lumber, and West Virginia coal to the factories in the Northeast. Illinois corn, California fruit, Kansas cattle, Iowa pigs, and western wheat were shipped on the railroad lines to the dinnerplates of Eastern factory workers. The west helped feed the growth of eastern industry.

 **GROWTH, HOWEVER, DID NOT COME WITHOUT COSTS.**

The indigenous peoples who lived in the west were forcibly removed to make way for American expansion. Many bloody conflicts came as a result of the American push westward.

The railroads were expensive to build and operate. Blasting through mountains and laying down tons of steel rail was not cheap, and railroads could take years to generate any profit. This meant that railroads required a large *initial investment*.

Because of this, railroads would play a huge role in the development of the American finance industry. Because the railroads needed investment capital, railroads would use the magic of *stocks* and *bonds* to turn average people around the globe into railroad investors. The railroad helped create the American stock market as we know it.

STOCKS AND BONDS

Remember your brownie business? Let's say you want to raise money to buy your ingredients. This means you want to raise *investment capital*. You might sell a *bond*. A bond is a lot like an IOU.

Somebody buys your brownie bond, you use the money to get your business going, and then you pay that person back (plus a little extra) over time.

But you might not be interested in carrying a loan, which is what a bond would be. Instead, you might do something totally different. You might ask your sibling to buy half the ingredients in exchange for half of the profit you make when you sell the brownies. Believe it or not, you have just sold a *share of stock* (often just called a "stock").

When you own stock in a company, you own a small part of that company. Companies try to reward stockholders by either attempting to *increase the price of each share* (how much somebody else will pay you to buy out your share of the company) or by declaring *dividends* (they distribute some part of their profits to the shareholders).

Railroads were pioneering in one final way: they were some of America's first big businesses. With offices and roads spanning the nation, railroads were truly massive enterprises. Many railroad companies, including the Pennsylvania Railroad, would "buy out" and absorb competitors to increase their spread over the continent.

If you have played the game of Monopoly (a game whose origins date to this era), you know this story well. After all, the point of the game is to create "monopolies": to get rid of your competition by owning all the utilities, railroads, or housing on a particular block.

FOR CONSUMERS, THIS CAN BE DISASTROUS.

But for businesses, forming a monopoly has benefits. Because there is nobody to compete with your company, you get the power to charge whatever you want. (Once you control every stall at the bake sale, there are no competitors. You can set the price of brownies at whatever you desire!) For this reason, many companies, ranging from oil and steel to sugar and railroads, attempted to form powerful monopolies in this time.

Railroads themselves may no longer play such an important role in our economy. But the changes they introduced—from the creation of big business to the development of American finance—are still with us!

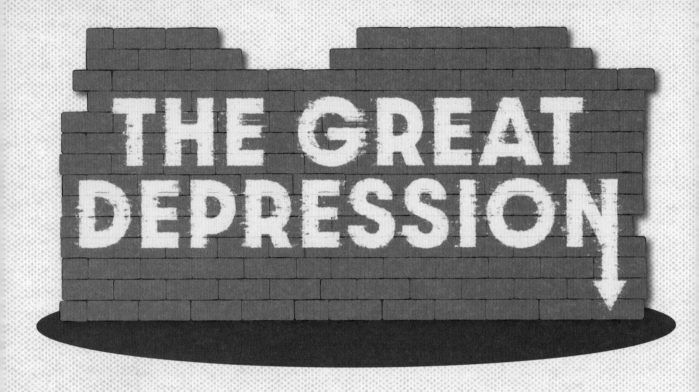

THE GREAT DEPRESSION

Does your family have an old story that everyone tells in a slightly different way? Someone tells that story about how your careless uncle once nearly burned down the family farm, and what does he say?

"WELL, *I* REMEMBER IT DIFFERENTLY!"

In much the same way, historians too often debate the past: they debate "what exactly happened."

And, as it turns out, much like those old family stories, there are many different stories historians tell about the origins of the Great Depression that began in 1929. What caused this massive economic crash? Different historians offer different answers to that question. Which one do you find most compelling?

MAYBE EVERYONE JUST GOT A BIT TOO EXCITED?

What is a share of stock worth? For one last time, let's return to your brownie business. Imagine that your sibling wanted to sell the 50% share you sold them just a chapter ago. How much would that "share" be worth? The answer is simple: *it is worth as much as somebody else is willing to pay for it!* And, believe it or not, the same is true of the larger American stock market. The stock price of any major company is determined by how much the next person is willing to pay to buy a share.

CHAPTER 8

This has a fascinating consequence: stock prices can soar because people are excited or confident. But on the flipside, stock prices can crash because people are scared or fearful!

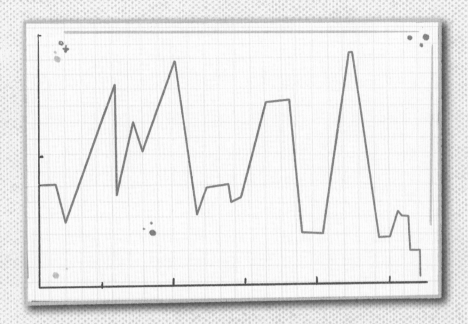

In the buildup to the Great Depression, there was great confidence in the markets. Stock prices were soaring. And as stock prices ticked upward, people got even more excited about buying stock, which only pushed prices up more. Many made great fortunes, at least for a while.

These high stock prices were not sustainable. In October 1929, the bubble burst. Stock prices plummeted. People rushed to sell their stocks. Excitement gave way to fear. Fortunes were lost. The Great Depression was upon us.

MAYBE POVERTY WAS THE PROBLEM?

Some historians think the stock market was not quite so important to the Depression. After all, few Americans actually owned any stock in this era. Most Americans

WILL WORK FOR FOOD.

were still farmers or workers. For these Americans, the decade leading up to the Great Depression was not a particularly good time. Farmers and workers were struggling. Factories were closing. Farms were failing.

WHAT KEEPS OUR ECONOMY GOING?

People spend money for the products they want! But most working Americans didn't have much money to spend, and those who lost their jobs had nothing to spend. It may seem obvious, but if people are too poor to buy anything, the economy comes to a halt. Following the Great Depression, many economists concluded that this awful cycle is what made this economic crash so devastating. Poverty caused economic distress, which just generated more poverty.

MAYBE BANKS WERE THE PROBLEM?

For other historians, the real cause of the Great Depression was the wave of *bank failures* that occurred during the early 1930s. Remember, banks only hold on to a small portion of the deposits they receive. The rest is loaned out. During the Great Depression, as the economic news grew increasingly grim, scared depositors rushed to local banks to withdraw their money: this was the

infamous "bank run" in action. The result? From 1930 to 1933, 10,000 banks in the United States failed. Billions of dollars were lost. Loaning stopped. The financial economy ground to a standstill.

FARMERS IN THE MIDWEST BURNED "USELESS" FOOD FOR HEAT WHILE UNEMPLOYED FACTORY WORKERS IN THE EAST WERE LEFT LITERALLY STARVING.

Historians argue over which story best explains the cause of the Great Depression because they each suggest a different

REMEMBER, AS WE HAVE LEARNED, NO BANK CAN PAY OFF ITS DEPOSITORS IF THEY ALL SHOW UP AT ONCE: MOST OF THE MONEY IS LOANED OUT, AFTER ALL. SO, IF ALL THE DEPOSITORS RUSH TO WITHDRAW THEIR MONEY IN A PANIC, THE BANK COLLAPSES.

solution for preventing future crises. If you think the Depression was caused by overconfident stock purchases, then you might want to better regulate the stock market. If you think the problem was poverty, then you might want to enact programs that help support the poor. If the problem was unstable banks, then you might want to beef up how our government supports or regulates the banking industry.

Whatever the cause, the result was an economy thrown into crisis. The percentage of workers without a job—the unemployment rate—soared. It hit nearly 25%, and it remained over 15% for much of the 1930s. Misery and poverty were everywhere. Jobs were almost impossible to find. Giant camps of homeless Americans sprung up around cities and towns. Americans became obsessed with a critical question:

HOW WOULD WE END THE GREAT DEPRESSION?

REBUILDING THE AMERICAN ECONOMY

In 1932, Franklin Delano Roosevelt rode into the presidency promising a "New Deal" to combat the Great Depression. His plan was to use the power of government to help restart the American economy. Early on, Roosevelt was willing to try just about anything if he thought it would help.

Eventually, however, his advisors urged him to embrace the programs laid out by an economist named John Maynard Keynes. (Pronounce his last name like "cains.")

KEYNES AND THE ECONOMY

What is the "economy," exactly? The "economy" is sort of like a big spider web connecting all of us together. We are each connected by the things we buy and sell. Let's say your mom is a doctor, and she buys you a new toy for $10. That toymaker then uses the $10 to buy a burrito. The burrito maker then uses that money to buy a history book. The overjoyed history book author then spends the $10 to buy a ticket to the county fair—where he immediately slips in the mud, throws out his back, and has to go to your mother's office to get fixed up. Through the magic of the economy, the money your mother spent on that toy came back to her! When seen in this way, you realize that every purchase you make helps keep the whole economy going. Connected together, we all support one another.

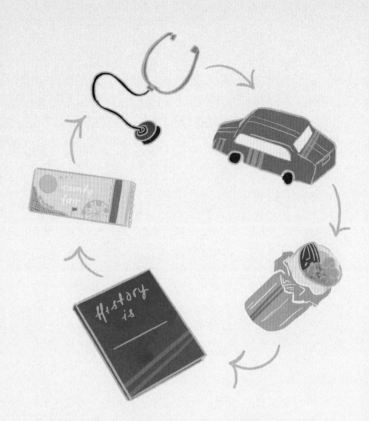

But this also means that if some of the strands of the web break, then the whole thing can fall apart. If the toymaker loses their job, they probably won't buy a burrito, which means the burrito maker would not have the money to buy a book, which means the author would never go to the fair, which means your mother would never get paid for fixing that poor author's busted back!

Economists such as Keynes saw this insight as important to understanding the Great Depression. Poor and unemployed people had no money to spend. When they stopped spending, this rippled throughout the whole economic web. People could not afford manufactured

products, so factories didn't sell anything and went out of business. Unemployed factory workers had no money for food, so farms failed. The web began to unravel.

This also meant that the problem could be fixed. The key, these "Keynesian" economists argued, was to use the power of the government to put money back into people's pockets. For instance, the government could temporarily hire workers to build roads or pay scientists to create innovations. This would benefit our economy with better

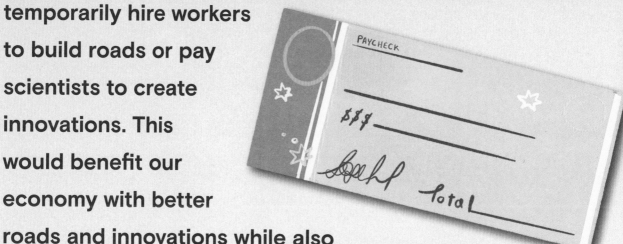

roads and innovations while also giving these newly employed Americans money to spend. And as these road-builders and scientists used their paychecks to buy the things they needed, others would reopen their businesses and rehire their workers to serve them.

THE ECONOMIC WEB WOULD BE MENDED AND THE ECONOMY WOULD BEGIN TO GROW AGAIN.

Roosevelt soon faced a key event that forced him to embrace Keynes's ideas: World War II. Confronted with global war, the government *had* to spend money and put people back to work making vehicles, weapons, ammunition, and planes. Government spending skyrocketed. And this government spending worked much like Keynes had predicted. As military factories popped up all over the United States, incomes shot up and the unemployment rate spiraled down. The Great Depression ended almost overnight.

World War II persuaded many policymakers that Keynes had it right. In the decades that followed, the government would use Keynesian policies to support the well-being of average people. Their spending, the idea went, would help support the entire economy.

JOHN MAYNARD KEYNES

Not everyone shared in this prosperity. While government policymakers were busy supporting economic growth by making it easier for average Americans to buy homes, go to college, invent new technologies, and get better wages, they often designed these programs to help white men. Women and African Americans were excluded from many important benefits. Thankfully, in recent decades, these groups have fought hard to get access to many of the benefits, jobs, and programs to which they were originally denied.

The era after World War II became a time of tremendous economic growth. Overall, the economy grew faster in the 1940s, 1950s, and 1960s than it has grown since. Incomes surged. Poverty declined. The United States became a true economic superpower.

THE RISE OF HIGH TECHNOLOGY

We think of the computer innovations of the last 75 years as springing from the workshops of individual inventors, but the reality is quite different. In fact, the foundation for this technological revolution was set by US government efforts to strengthen our economy and military after World War II. Take, for instance, the first true electronic computer: the Electronic Numerical Integrator and Computer (ENIAC).

Completed in 1946, the computer was funded by the US Army. Its goal was to help with firing missiles. The ENIAC weighed about as much as 20 cars and had to be housed in a 30-by-50-foot room!

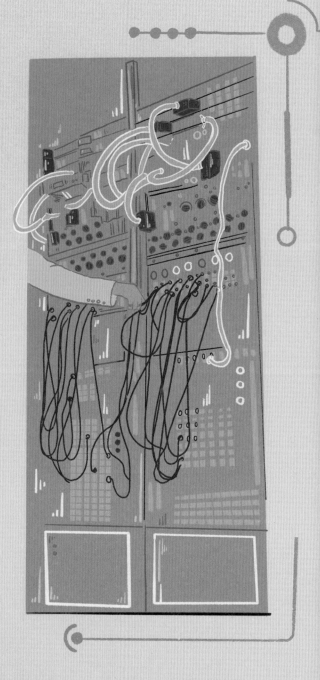

But it was a start. So many important technologies today have similar stories. They started at government-funded labs at universities and corporations. Today's "internet," for example, started as the ARPANET, created to link together the nation's military research labs. Government spending on research also brought us virtual reality, nuclear power, rocketry, wireless communications, space travel, and global positioning, among other technological innovations.

THE RISE OF COMPUTING AND DIGITAL COMMUNICATIONS COMPLETELY CHANGED OUR ECONOMY.

Companies now use computers to track nearly every aspect of business: sales, inventory, investment, purchasing, profits, shipping, and more. Manufacturers spanning the globe can network together to work in unison, often through the use of computerized machinery. There are nearly three million industrial robots operating in the world today. On farms, some tractors can drive themselves through the use of global positioning satellites, and they use digital sensors that track soil and climate conditions.

Beginning in the 1970s, the US government cut how much it spends on technological development. Some now worry that this is slowing technological growth. Some people notice that many recent "innovations" are not really innovations at all, but instead sleeker or smaller versions of existing technologies.

GOVERNMENT + SCIENCE

When nuclear power for electricity launched in the 1950s, it was like nothing the world had ever seen before. In contrast, while a "smartphone" may seem amazing, the technologies it uses have actually been around for decades. Are we living at the end of an exciting era of technological growth?

Many people disagree with this belief. They argue that we have simply entered a new era in which individuals and businesses are taking the lead in technological improvement. There are certainly examples of this. Bill Gates, a college dropout with a passion for computers, founded Microsoft in 1975. By the 1980s his company was already a leading software producer. By the 1990s, Gates was the richest person in the world. From Elon Musk to Jeff Bezos, there are many wealthy tech "stars" in America today.

Whatever position you might take, it is hard not to marvel at how much these recent technological changes have transformed our lives.

ENDURING DEBATES

In the 1970s, a seemingly small thing happened that had enormous consequences: the price of oil (and with it, gas) shot up. In about a decade, oil prices jumped 800%. Gas was scarce. Cars lined up outside of gas stations. Americans clamored for the now precious resource.

Why did increasing prices at the gas pump change the American economy? It caused *price inflation*. Remember, even today, just about everything requires gas to get from producer to consumer. So, as companies had to pay more to transport  their goods, they raised the prices of those goods to make up for that change. Pretty soon, the prices Americans were paying for everything (not just gas) started to shoot up. When the average price of goods in the economy goes up, we call it *inflation*; when it goes down, we call it *deflation*.

The 1970s became defined by massive inflation. As prices surged, people stopped spending as much. The economy slowed. Unemployment started to creep up.

As Americans sought relief from increasing prices and slowing economic growth, many in Washington, D.C., embraced a new economic ideology. It was called *Neoliberalism*, and it was different from the ideas proposed during the Great Depression. Keynesian economists had blamed the Great Depression on a lack of *consumer spending*. Neoliberals, however, saw the opposite issue at play: a lack of *investment capital*. In other words, the problem was not that average Americans lacked money in their pockets to spend. The problem was that business operators were being held back by government rules, regulations, and taxes.

PRESIDENT RONALD REAGAN

As one of America's most famous Neoliberals, President Ronald Reagan, put it in his inaugural address,

> **"GOVERNMENT IS NOT THE SOLUTION TO OUR PROBLEM, GOVERNMENT *IS* THE PROBLEM."**

Coming into office in 1980, Reagan cut environmental laws and protections, cut many social welfare programs, and cut taxes (especially on corporations). With less government interference and taxation, the idea went, American business would have more freedom to invest, innovate, and increase growth.

DID REAGAN'S REFORMS WORK?

It depends who you ask! For Neoliberals, Reagan's reforms got business leaders excited to reinvest in America. Inflation slowed and economic growth restarted.

Keynesians see things differently. They point out that these cuts to government programs, paired with tax cuts that mostly benefited the already quite wealthy, actually slowed down economic growth and worsened economic inequality. After all, in recent years, the richest Americans have grown much richer while incomes for everyone else have mostly remained the same.

These may seem like old debates, but they still play an enormous role in our current politics. Today's "Democratic Party" continues to push for Keynes's basic policies. In the relief bills Democrats passed in response to the COVID-19 pandemic, for example, we saw so many things that would have met with Keynes's approval. One of the key features of these programs was the government sending money to every American.

"Yes!," Keynes might say.

> **"THAT IS HOW YOU FIX AN ECONOMY! MAKE SURE PEOPLE HAVE MONEY IN THEIR POCKETS TO SPEND. THEY WILL BUY THE THINGS THEY WANT AND, IN TURN, JUMPSTART ECONOMIC GROWTH!"**

Today's Republican Party is home to those who oppose these ideas. Republicans, however, are a bit more divided. Many still embrace Neoliberalism. "No!," they might say.

> **"CUTTING CHECKS TO EVERY AMERICAN WILL JUST DRIVE UP GOVERNMENT DEBT AND INFLATION. INSTEAD, WE NEED TO CUT TAXES AND SLASH THE REGULATIONS THAT ARE HOLDING BACK THE ENGINES OF AMERICAN INNOVATION!"**

Other Republicans suggest mixing these Neoliberal ideas with an older set of proposals that go back to Alexander Hamilton. Some talk of increasing tariffs (taxes on imports) and decreasing immigration in an attempt to help struggling American industries. Massive tariffs, immigration restriction, cutting business regulations, cutting taxes, and cutting social welfare programs are some of the

hallmarks of this line of thinking. Rather than taking a hands-off approach, the hope is that aggressive government investment in business will pay off for all Americans.

You would not be alone if you are at times surprised by how much anger these debates can stir up. But, remember, much of what makes Americans so invested in this or that set of political beliefs is that we all actually agree on something critical: the economy is important! We all want to see an America with a growing and sustainable economy that promises prosperity to everyone. Many of us disagree on how to achieve